Under The Grammar Hammer

The 25 Most Important Grammar Mistakes
and
How to Avoid Them

Douglas Cazort

Lowell House
Los Angeles
Contemporary Books
Chicago

Library of Congress Cataloging-in-Publication Data
Cazort, Douglas.
    Under the grammar hammer : the 25 most important grammar mistakes and how
to avoid them / Douglas Cazort.
        p. cm.
    Includes bibliographical references and index.
    ISBN 0-929923-75-8
    1. English language—Errors of usage.   2. English language—Grammar—
1950– I. Title.
PE1460.C33   1992
428.2—dc20   92-2774
                                                                                          CIP

Requests for such permissions should be addressed to:
Lowell House
2029 Century Park East, Suite 3290
Los Angeles, CA 90067
Publisher: Jack Artenstein
Executive Vice-President: Nick Clemente
Vice-President/Editor-in-Chief: Janice Gallagher
Design: Hespenheide Design
Illustrations: Will Suckow
Manufactured in the United States of America
10 9 8 7 6 5 4 3 2 1

Contents

▼▼▼▼▼▼▼▼▼

Celebrating 500 Years of Modern Language Grammar Books

Ask any school child what happened in 1492, and what answer will you get? That's right, "Columbus sailed the ocean blue." But the truly earthshaking event to come out of Spain that year was the publication of the first grammar of any modern European language. Laugh if you will, folks, but this is the 500th anniversary of grammar books, a fine tradition kicked off by the same people who brought you Christopher Columbus and the Spanish Inquisition.

After your own experience with grammar in school and at work, some of you might see a sinister intent to inflict pain weaving its way through all these Spanish innovations. And as farfetched as it may sound, there may have been a connection between grammar books and the 15th-century Spanish desire for world domination. Hard to believe? Well, listen to this.

In 1492, when the Bishop of Avila presented Queen Isabella of Spain with a copy of the first grammar, the queen asked what it was for.

"Your Majesty," the bishop replied, "language is the perfect instrument of empire" (Peter Farb, *Word Play,* page 157).

So what does this have to do with you today, 500 years and 5,000 grammar books later? Well, I'm no bishop, that's for sure, and I don't make any imperial claims for *Under the Grammar Hammer,* though there's a case to be made for the economic benefits of a literate population. But I have to dedicate this book to someone, and we don't have a monarch who rules an empire beyond the seas. So I'll settle for the First Lady of the land, Barbara Bush, and dedicate this book to her in recognition of her work in literacy, with the hope that my small contribution will make a difference in greater economic progress, both the nation's and my own.

And while I'm at it, I'd like to include my parents, John Cazort and Carolyn McMullen Cazort, who gave me a love of books and words; and my wife, Connie Layman Cazort, and our son, Max, who continue to give me a love of life.

Acknowledgments

I'd like to thank Janice Gallagher and Nomi Kleinmuntz, my first editors at Lowell House, for asking me to write this book, and Lee Ann Leeson, director of Composition at Pepperdine University, for sending them my way. Others at Pepperdine who helped me with research or manuscript preparation were: Ray Hileman, Brad Johnson, Kirstin Landt, Michelle Bragg, Sue Bauer, Glenn Briggs, and Mary Sumner. I'd also like to thank the people who took part as subjects in the research: Ted Ridlehuber and Jim Knauf of Canon Financial Institute and the participants in their 1991 Pepperdine seminar; the English teachers who attended the 1991 Regional Writing Conference at Pepperdine; and members of the Pepperdine faculty and staff. Finally, I want to give credit to Betsy Amster at Lowell House, who left her mark on every page of this book.

1

Who's Afraid of the Grammar Hammer?

▼▼▼▼▼▼▼▼▼

Picture yourself at a party, talking to someone new. You get around to asking each other what you do for a living, and your new acquaintance says, "I'm an English teacher." What effect does that have on the care you take with your speech? Do you feel nervous about the possibility of making mistakes in grammar?

If not, try this situation on for size: You're applying for a job, and your prospective employer wants you to write a one-page statement of your goals in life and how they fit the needs of the firm. Would you feel any reluctance to writing it, any fear that grammar will come between you and success?

If you would feel all right in the above situations, then you are in a minority in American society. Most of us feel uncomfortable with writing and the people who teach it. We're convinced we cannot write well. We even hate writing. In a survey conducted by Morris Holland, a professor of psychology at UCLA, 80 percent of UCLA students surveyed had avoided courses, major fields of study, or careers that require writing. If those figures are true for the highly literate population on a college campus such as UCLA, what would the figures be for the population at large? I would guess even greater. What's the reason for this widespread linguistic anxiety? The following stories may point to some of the causes.

When people find out I teach English for a living, they often laugh nervously and say they had better watch their grammar. Then, many tell me a grammar horror story.

Recently, a lawyer who works for a bank added this one to my collection. An employee at the bank sent a letter containing several mistakes to one of the bank's best customers. After red-marking the mistakes, the customer sent the letter back with the following comment written across the bottom: "Fifteen mistakes in twenty words. Don't you think that's a bit much?" Shortly thereafter, the bank manager fired the employee, citing the letter as one of the major causes.

Another story comes from an editor at a publishing house. She said that a friend of hers who works for another publisher asked her to consider hiring his son as an editorial assistant. The son came for an interview and impressed the editor as a go-getting, take-charge type of guy. However, when the editor read his résumé, she found several errors in typing and grammar, so she didn't give him the job. How many errors?

"Two or three," the editor told me. "In this business, that's too many."

Often people recount stories of receiving red marks and low grades that still rankle years later. One friend told me about a high school teacher who took one of his papers, shredded it into a plastic bag like the ones people use to clean up while walking their dogs, and told the class that the paper was equal in quality to what the bag normally contained.

Perhaps the most painful story I've heard of comes from Richard Gentry's book, *Spel Is a Four-Letter Word*. In it, he tells of a person whose fifth-grade teacher would make her kneel on hard, uncooked rice whenever she made five mistakes in spelling. Ouch!

These stories vary from person to person, but they carry a common message. In many situations, we have good reason to feel uncomfortable using our own language. We have been red-marked, graded down, not hired, and even fired for mistakes in grammar and spelling. And the situation isn't likely to change in the near future. Surveys show that many Americans react strongly to mistakes in writing.

What can we do about it? One professor of English has proposed a solution with far-reaching social implications: "If you can't spell, marry someone who can." I propose a simpler solution: Buy this book. Reading it will teach you the most common mistakes in writing that educated Americans make, and what's more important, which mistakes are the most serious (the kind that will get you fired at the bank). I often call this body of rules and conventions the "grammar hammer." When you swing it and miss, you can deliver a nasty blow to your thumb. Sometimes, you may feel you are *all* thumbs, and each and every one of them is bruised and swollen.

To help improve your swing, we'll look at the misses that cause the most frequent and serious bruises, and then we'll learn rules of thumb to keep all your fingers out of the grammar hammer's range.

At the same time, I hope to free you from the idea that the
English language is the sole property of English teachers and
other authorities on correct usage. It belongs to all of us who
use it, and part of my purpose in writing this book is to help
you feel more secure in your ownership, even in the presence
of English teachers.

2

Getting the Most for Your Money
from this Book

▼▼▼▼▼▼▼▼▼

This will sound strange coming from the author of a grammar handbook, but the world doesn't really need another grammar handbook. The market already offers an adequate supply. What the world needs now is a book that pulls together the most important grammar rules and presents them so you can learn them quickly and easily.

Viewed from another perspective, we need a grammar handbook that applies the 80/20 rule, a principle derived by Vilfredo Pareto, an Italian mathematician and economist. The rule states that in any process or task, 80 percent of the problems are a result of 20 percent of the causes (Walton, *Deming Management at Work,* page 24). Applying the rule to the study of grammar, we would focus on the 20 percent of the mistakes that we commit 80 percent of the time. In other words, we need a grammar handbook that shows us how to deal with the few mistakes we make most often.

By now, I'll bet you have guessed that this is the book, right? Well, with all due modesty, I must say you are correct. This is an 80/20 book from start to finish. In fact, it focuses on the 20 most common mistakes that educated Americans make, and it ranks them in order of their seriousness (with 5 uncommon but very serious mistakes thrown in for free).

How do I know that these 20 mistakes are the ones we make most often? Because a nationwide study by Professors Andrea Lunsford of Ohio State University and Robert Connors of the University of New Hampshire found them to be the most common mistakes in college student writing. And what do I mean by the "seriousness" of a mistake? As Professor Maxine Hairston of the University of Texas puts it, "Not all errors are created equal." Some will pass unnoticed, while some will get you fired at the bank. Research tells us which types of mistakes bother Americans very little and which bother them a lot. Hairston did the original research in 1979; I followed it up with a study in 1991.

Combining all this research, we get the 20 most common mistakes arranged in order of seriousness (again with 5 uncommon but serious mistakes thrown in for free). This combination gives you the option to focus your efforts where they will count the most. And this brings us back to the purpose of this section: How do you get the most for your money from this book?

Once again, follow the 80/20 rule. Read through the "Sneak Previews" to find out which mistakes cause you the most problems and which do not. Then move to the expanded sections ("Grammar's Top 20 Misses" and "Five Uncommonly Serious Mistakes") and tackle your problem errors in the order they are arranged, starting with the most serious, ending with the least. If you like, don't bother reading the sections that deal with mistakes you don't make. To your pleasant surprise, you may find you don't need to learn as much as you thought to boost your confidence in your control of grammar. That's my hope for you, anyway, and I also hope you'll have some fun while you're using this book.

So, pick up that hammer and take aim. The journey of 1,000 hits begins with a single swing.

3

Sneak Preview: Grammar's Top 20 Misses (From Most Serious to Least)

▼▼▼▼▼▼▼▼▼

Step right up, folks. For your viewing pleasure, here is the minimum information you need for maximum returns on your effort. In this sneak preview and the next, I'll name each mistake, give a sample sentence that contains it, and then show a corrected version of the sentence. But first, one word of warning: Don't let the grammar terms scare you off. Even if you never learn the name of each mistake, you'll still be able to recognize it and avoid making it. And then, after seeing examples and reading the definitions in the expanded sections, you'll absorb the terminology whether you intend to or not.

So, leave your worries at the theater door, sit back, relax, and enjoy the show.

1. Wrong Tense or Verb Form

Bad Swing: When William the Conqueror invaded England in 1066, he *done* the English language a big favor.

Direct Hit: When William the Conqueror invaded England in 1066, he *did* the English language a big favor.

2. Fused or Run-on Sentence

Bad Swing: Over 75 percent of mistakes in English cannot be committed in speech they can only be made in writing.

Direct Hit: Over 75 percent of mistakes in English cannot be committed in speech. They can only be made in writing.

3. Sentence Fragment

Bad Swing: With 500,000 words, the English vocabulary is larger than that of any other language. *Partly because 80 percent of English words come from foreign sources.*

Direct Hit: With 500,000 words, the English vocabulary is larger than that of any other language, partly because 80 percent of English words come from foreign sources.

4. Lack of Agreement Between Subject and Verb

Bad Swing: An important function of managers *are* delegating responsibility.

Direct Hit: An important function of managers *is* delegating responsibility.

5. Wrong Word

Bad Swing: Creative people believe *their* creative.

Direct Hit: Creative people believe *they're* creative.

6. Missing Comma(s) with a Nonrestrictive Element

Bad Swing: Roger von Oech's *A Whack on the Side of the Head* expanded and revised for the 1990s is an excellent guide to a more creative life.

Direct Hit: Roger von Oech's *A Whack on the Side of the Head,* expanded and revised for the 1990s, is an excellent guide to a more creative life.

7. Unnecessary Shift in Tense

Bad Swing: The first English dictionary was published in 1604 and written by Robert Cawdray, who *says* he produced it for "ladies . . . and other unskillful persons."

Direct Hit: The first English dictionary was published in 1604 and written by Robert Cawdray, who *said* he produced it for "ladies . . . and other unskillful persons."

8. Missing Commas in a Series

Bad Swing: George Burns defines happiness as having a large loving caring close-knit family in another city.

Direct Hit: George Burns defines happiness as having a large, loving, caring, close-knit family in another city.

9. Missing or Misplaced Possessive Apostrophe

Bad Swing: Parkinsons Law states that a job expands to fill the allotted time.

Direct Hit: Parkinson's Law states that a job expands to fill the allotted time.

10. Unnecessary Comma(s) with a Restrictive Element

Bad Swing: Linguistic research has found, that New Yorkers communicate social class through their pronunciation of the letter *r*.

Direct Hit: Linguistic research has found that New Yorkers communicate social class through their pronunciation of the letter *r*.

11. Confusion of *Its* and *It's*

Bad Swing: "If it sells, *its* creative," they say in advertising.

Direct Hit: "If it sells, *it's* creative," they say in advertising.

12. Dangling or Misplaced Modifier

Bad Swing: *Popping, sparking, and blowing fuses,* the CEO stood helplessly watching at the podium while the new audio-visual system self-destructed.

Direct Hit: Popping, sparking, and blowing fuses, the new audio-visual system self-destructed while the CEO stood helplessly watching at the podium.

13. Lack of Agreement Between Pronoun and Antecedent

Bad Swing: A "Type-A" *person* will hurry *themselves* to death.

Direct Hit: "Type-A" *people* will hurry *themselves* to death.

14. Wrong or Missing Preposition

Bad Swing: We need to invent a language in which politicians would be incapable *from* lying.

Direct Hit: We need to invent a language in which politicians would be incapable *of* lying.

15. Vague Pronoun Reference

Bad Swing: Some managers focus only on short-term profit, *which* can lower the quality of the product or service.

Direct Hit: Some managers focus only on short-term profit, a practice that can lower the quality of the product or service.

16. Unnecessary Shift in Pronoun

Bad Swing: If *one* wants to become an international airline pilot, *they* have to learn English.

Direct Hit: If *you* want to become an international airline pilot, *you* have to learn English.

17. Comma Splice

Bad Swing: Professor Adams Sherman Hill of Harvard was obsessed with mistakes in spelling and grammar, he passed his obsession on to generations of English teachers and the American public.

Direct Hit: Professor Adams Sherman Hill of Harvard was obsessed with mistakes in spelling and grammar, *and* he passed his obsession on to generations of English teachers and the American public.

18. Wrong or Missing Verb Ending

Bad Swing: The healthy office worker *park* one mile from work and *walk* twenty minutes for exercise.

Direct Hit: The healthy office worker *parks* one mile from work and *walks* twenty minutes for exercise.

19. Missing Commas in a Compound Sentence

Bad Swing: Many Americans own a thesaurus yet these books of synonyms don't exist for some languages with small vocabularies.

Direct Hit: Many Americans own a thesaurus, yet these books of synonyms don't exist for some languages with small vocabularies.

20. Missing Comma After an Introductory Element

Bad Swing: While the dog ate the cat stayed away from the dish.

Direct Hit: While the dog ate, the cat stayed away from the dish.

4

Sneak Preview: Five Uncommonly Serious Mistakes

▼▼▼▼▼▼▼▼▼

The following 5 mistakes are not among the 20 most common, but they receive strong negative responses when committed. In other words, we don't make these mistakes very often, but when we do, we cause strong negative reactions. Once again, use this section as a self-test. If you don't make these mistakes, forget them. If you do, take steps to get rid of them.

1. Objective Case Pronouns Used as Subjects

Bad Swing: Her guru and *her* agreed that we are what we think.

Direct Hit: Her guru and *she* agreed that we are what we think.

2. Double Negatives

Bad Swing: One hard lesson for many to learn is that worry wo*n't hardly* change the future.

Direct Hit: One hard lesson for many to learn is that worry will hardly change the future.

3. Failure to Capitalize Proper Names

Bad Swing: roger von oech, the president of creative think, has conducted workshops on creativity for american express, apple computer, procter and gamble, and the japanese management association.

Direct Hit: Roger von Oech, the president of Creative Think, has conducted workshops on creativity for American Express, Apple Computer, Procter and Gamble, and the Japanese Management Association.

4. Faulty Parallelism

Bad Swing: A good manager requires the ability to lead, the capacity to learn, and *delegating.*

Direct Hit: A good manager requires the ability to lead, the capacity to learn, and the willingness *to delegate.*

5. Subjective-Case Pronouns Used as Objects

Bad Swing: The senator's use of double negatives surprised my students and *I*.

Direct Hit: The senator's use of double negatives surprised my students and *me*.

5

You Know More Grammar than You Know You Know, and You Need to Learn Less than You Think

▼▼▼▼▼▼▼▼

As you leaf through this book, a question may occur to you about the number of grammar terms you'll find, or actually, *won't* find. Why so few? I'm glad you asked.

I want to use the smallest number of terms necessary to keep your thumbs dancing nimbly out from under the grammar hammer. Most of what you need to know can be taught by example, without requiring you to scale a mountain of terminology.

To make the point I'm making here, Patrick Hartwell, a professor of English at Indiana University of Pennsylvania, performs this simple experiment: He asks people to state the rule in English grammar that determines the placement order of adjectives of nationality, age, and number before a noun.

"Whaaat?" you may answer. "I don't even understand the question, much less know the rule."

That's about the way I responded, as did my wife (also a teacher), and our twelve-year-old son, and all the people Hartwell asks. Then Hartwell asks the same people to place the following words in their normal order:

French   the   young   girls   four

Please take a minute to reorder them yourself. Don't worry about the time. I'll wait.

If you arranged the words as I did (and my wife, son, and all of Hartwell's respondents), you came up with "the four young French girls," even though you claimed not to know the rule. And to arrive at your answer, did you first have to consciously learn that the rule in English for the order of these adjectives is number, age, and nationality? In the words of Homey the Clown, "I don't *think* so."

The strange thing about the vast majority of the grammar rules that generate a language is that you don't need to know them consciously in order to use the language correctly. There's a good analogy here with running. In order to run a marathon, you don't need to take a course in physiology and learn the names and functions of all the muscles and bones in your legs. You just need to go out and jog a number of miles every day for a year. Then, along the way, you may need to know the word *ankle*, but not much else, when you go to the doctor to tell her what you sprained.

Likewise, with English, you need to hear it and read it in its standard form to use it correctly, with a few trips to the grammar doctor to fix some mistakes. And so, my friends, proceed, for the doctor is in.

6

Grammar's Top 20 Misses (From Most Serious to Least)

▼▼▼▼▼▼▼▼▼

All right, folks, now that you have finished the Sneak Previews, you're ready for the full catastrophe. In the following chapters, you'll see Bad Swings and Direct Hits (just as you did in the Sneak Previews), but now, for your further edification, you'll get the whole story of each mistake packaged neatly in boxes and followed by the Rules of Thumb for keeping all your fingers out from under the grammar hammer.

So, move over, Paula Abdul, because here comes the real thing.

1. Wrong Tense or Verb Form

Bad Swing: When William the Conqueror invaded England
                in 1066, he *done* the English language a big
                favor.

Direct Hit: When William the Conqueror invaded England
                in 1066, he *did* the English language a big
                favor.

Bad Swing: Along with his army and court, King William
                brung the French language, which contributed
                over 10,000 words to English between 1100
                and 1500.

Direct Hit: Along with his army and court, King William
                brought the French language, which
                contributed over 10,000 words to English
                between 1100 and 1500.

Verbs, Social Status, and Crime

Using the wrong verb form causes the strongest reaction
of any of the top 20 errors because this error constitutes
what linguists call a "status marker." That means that it
belongs to a type of error that causes us to assign a lower
social status to its user. For example, when we hear people
say, "we was" or "he don't," we consider them uneducated, "lower class," or even criminal. Yes, criminal. The
next time you see a TV or movie rendition of street crime,
listen to the bad guys' use of verbs. Regardless of the color
of their skin or nature of their crimes, usually if they don't
say *ain't*, they ain't no criminal. (Revised: If they don't say
ain't, they aren't criminals.) So watch your verbs, or you
may end up in the grammar slammer.

Rules of Thumb

▲ RULE #1:

Write first; edit later.

I'll repeat this rule in every section because it is as important as any of the grammar rules you will learn. Why? One problem with studying errors is that you may become *too* conscious of making them. Then, when you are writing, this very error consciousness may inhibit you, slowing you down and distracting your mind from where it needs to be. Instead of worrying about making mistakes, you need to be concentrating on getting your thoughts down on paper.

So, when you write, think of your readers and what you need to say to them to get your point across. If you aren't sure of a point of grammar or the spelling of a word, circle it and keep writing. Then, look it up later. How many times have you stopped in the middle of writing a sentence to check the spelling of a word, only to lose the idea for the rest of the sentence? Don't let that happen again. Write first; edit later.

▲ RULE #2:

When in doubt about the standard form of an irregular verb, look it up in a dictionary.

A *regular verb* forms its past tenses simply by adding *-ed* to the verb. For example, today I hammer a nail, yesterday I hammer*ed* a nail, and in the past, I have often hammer*ed* nails. No problem.

The major problem arises with *irregular verbs,* verbs that form their past tenses without using *-ed.* When you don't know the past tenses of an irregular verb, you can look in a dictionary to find the forms the verb takes in the present tense, past tense, and as a past participle. For example, look up *go* and you will find: **go,** went, gone. What does that tell you? That in the present, you *go,* yesterday you *went,* and often in the past, you have *gone* somewhere.

The problem with irregular verbs comes with the use of nonstandard forms of the past tense and past participle. If you have difficulty with any of these, proceed to Rule #3.

▲ RULE #3:

Learn the principal parts of the verbs listed below. Make up sentences that use them, write the sentences, and read them aloud. This is a partial list of the most problematic verbs, based on tests of students in my English classes. For a more complete list, see any grammar handbook or editing manual.

Today I:	Yesterday I:	In the past, I have:
am (from *to be*)	was (we were)	been
become	became	become
begin	began	begun
bend	bent	bent
bet	bet	bet
bite	bit	bitten (or) bit
bleed	bled	bled
blow	blew	blown
bring	brought	brought
burst	burst	burst
buy	bought	bought
cast	cast	cast
choose	chose	chosen
cling	clung	clung
cost	cost	cost
dig	dug	dug
dive	dived (or) dove	dived
drink	drank	drunk
drive	drove	driven
fling	flung	flung
fly	flew	flown
forbid	forbade	forbidden
forget	forgot	forgotten
freeze	froze	frozen
get	got	gotten
grind	ground	ground
hang	hung	hung
have	had	had
hurt	hurt	hurt
know	knew	known
lay	laid	laid
lend	lent	lent
lie	lay	lain
mistake	mistook	mistaken
ride	rode	ridden

ring	rang	rung
run	ran	run
see	saw	seen
seek	sought	sought
send	sent	sent
shake	shook	shaken
shine	shone	shone
shrink	shrank	shrunk
sing	sang	sung
sink	sank (or) sunk	sunk
slide	slid	slid
speak	spoke	spoken
spin	spun	spun
spring	sprang	sprung
sting	stung	stung
stink	stank	stunk
strike	struck	struck
swear	swore	sworn
swim	swam	swum
swing	swung	swung
take	took	taken
tear	tore	torn
think	thought	thought
throw	threw	thrown
wake	woke	waken
weep	wept	wept
wind	wound	wound
wring	wrung	wrung

2. Fused or Run-on Sentence

Bad Swing: Over 75 percent of mistakes in English cannot be committed in speech they can only be made in writing.

Direct Hit: Over 75 percent of mistakes in English cannot
be committed in speech. They can only be
made in writing.

Bad Swing: Professor W. E. Deming has enjoyed a varied
career as a physicist, mathematician, and
statistician he is now becoming famous as the
American who taught quality to the Japanese.

Direct Hit: Professor W. E. Deming has enjoyed a varied
career as a physicist, mathematician, and
statistician. He is now becoming famous as the
American who taught quality to the Japanese.

What Humans Hath Joined Together
We Must Sometimes Put Asunder
Fused or *run-on* sentences are two or more sentences
married without benefit of punctuation. The solution:
sentence divorce court. See Rules of Thumb for proper
proceedings.

**Rules of
Thumb**

▲ RULE #1:
_____

Write first; edit later.

▲ RULE #2:
_____

"De-fuse" this error in one of the following ways.

Separate the sentences with a period:

Direct Hit: Over 75 percent of mistakes in English cannot
              be committed in speech. They can only be
              made in writing.

Add a comma and a conjunction (*and, but, or, so, yet*):

Direct Hit: Professor W. E. Deming has enjoyed a varied
              career as a physicist, mathematician, and
              statistician, *and* he is now becoming famous as
              the American who taught quality to the
              Japanese.

Place a semicolon between the two sentences:

Direct Hit: Over 75 percent of mistakes in English cannot
              be committed in speech; they can only be
              made in writing.

Where it fits, transform one of the sentences into a *because*
clause:

Direct Hit: Over 75 percent of mistakes in English cannot
              be committed in speech *because* they can only
              be made in writing.

Punctuation: A Code for Writers Only

think about it when we speak we dont use punctuation marks or capitals but somehow we manage to understand each other without them if you have read this far without them you realize how much they help writers and readers and how frustrating and confusing their absence can be

Had enough? So have I, but you see my point. When we speak, we use many cues to "punctuate" what we are saying: voice tones, pauses, eye contact, facial expressions, hand movements, and the statements and questions of our cospeakers. But when we write, all these cues are missing. So, over the past 2,000 years, writers have developed a code that principally relies on punctuation, but also on capitalization and even indentation.

If you like spy stories about secret codes and code breakers, try to imagine you're learning a code to communicate with readers whenever you have to learn a new use of punctuation. Then, maybe it won't seem so daunting. If that doesn't make punctuation any easier for you, don't blame me for not trying.

---

3. Sentence Fragment

Bad Swing: With 500,000 words, the English vocabulary is larger than that of any other language. *Partly because 80 percent of English words come from foreign sources.*

Direct Hit: With 500,000 words, the English vocabulary is larger than that of any other language, **partly** because 80 percent of English words come from foreign sources.

Bad Swing: Professor W. E. Deming tells American businesses to export anything except American management. *At least not to a friendly country.*

Direct Hit: Professor W. E. Deming tells American
                businesses to export anything except
                American management, at least not to a
                friendly country.

Fragments: What They Are Is What They Aren't

A fragment can be defined in two ways: as what it isn't (a complete sentence), or as what it is (a phrase or clause incorrectly punctuated as a sentence). Read the following fragments and their revisions aloud, and train your ear to hear the difference. Then replace similar fragments in your own writing with the appropriate revisions.

**Rules of
Thumb**

▲ RULE #1:

Write first; edit later.

▲ RULE #2:

Eliminate the following types of fragments from your writing.

Bad Swing: Your work force is being molded right here. *In high schools where one out of every four students drop out. Where 61 percent of those remaining graduate with the belief that profit isn't a necessary part of running a business.*

Direct Hit: Your work force is being molded right here, in high schools where one out of every four students drop out, and 61 percent of those remaining graduate with the belief that profit isn't a necessary part of running a business.

Bad Swing: It comes down to this: students lacking exposure to the working world will continue to affect the quality of American business. *Your business. Unless more attention is paid to the problem.*

Direct Hit: It comes down to this: students lacking exposure to the working world will continue to affect the quality of American business, your business, unless more attention is paid to the problem.

The English Minor Sentence:
A Major Cause for Confusion

Just when you thought you knew the rules for avoiding sentence fragments, this comes along: There's such a thing as an *acceptable* fragment, or *intended* fragment, or as some grammarians call it, the English minor sentence. In other words, a fragment used intentionally for emphasis. Here's the catch. If you don't intend to use it, you have made a mistake. At least that's how some English teachers (as well as people in the "real" world) will explain why they won't let *you* write fragments even though you see them used in published writing.

To illustrate this no-man's land (or woman's either), I wrote one fragment (intentionally) in the previous paragraph. I also took the sample fragments in Rules of Thumb from an ad in *Time* (June 10, 1991). And I got the Deming sample fragment from *Dr. Deming,* a book written by Rafael Aguayo. Obviously, in many cases, it's all right to use fragments.

So, where does that leave you and *your* fragments? In the crossfire between pro- and anti-fragmentarians. What's my advice? Keep your head down. If you are a student whose teacher grades down for fragments, then edit them out of your rough drafts (Write first! Edit later!). If your work requires you to write, play it safe. Keep your sentences major and your worries minor. After all, we don't want you to get fired at the bank, not for minor sentences, anyway.

4. Lack of Agreement Between Subject and Verb

Bad Swing: An important function of managers *are* delegating responsibility.

Direct Hit: An important function of managers *is* delegating responsibility.

Bad Swing: Neither *Peking Man* nor *Neanderthal Man refer* to men alone.

Direct Hit: Neither *Peking Man* nor *Neanderthal Man refers* to men alone.

**Why Won't Subjects and Verbs
Agree *Not* to Disagree?**

How can a subject and verb disagree? What's to disagree about? Only number, my friends. In other words, a plural subject requires a plural verb, and a singular subject requires a singular verb. Normally, this presents no problem. We supply the correct form of the verb unconsciously. But in certain exceptional cases, we are fooled into providing the wrong forms. See the Rules of Thumb for the most common of these exceptions.

Rules of
Thumb

▲ RULE #1:
_____

Write first; edit later.

▲ RULE #2:
_____

Don't be tricked by words between the subject and the verb:

Direct Hit: An important function of poets is to re-create
our familiar world so that we can see it in an
unfamiliar light.
(The subject is *function*, not *poets*.)

▲ RULE #3:
_____

Subjects joined by *and* require a plural verb:

Direct Hit: An English teacher and a red pen *make* a
dangerous mix.

▲ RULE #4:
_____

When compound subjects are joined by *or, either . . . or,
neither . . . nor,* or *not only . . . but,* the verb agrees with the
nearer subject:

Direct Hit: Neither incorrect punctuation nor misspellings
appear as mistakes in spoken English.

Direct Hit: Neither misspellings nor incorrect punctuation
appears as a mistake in spoken English.

▲ RULE #5:

Amounts as subjects take a singular verb:

Direct Hit: One-hundred-thousand dollars *is* no longer a large salary for a professional athlete.

Direct Hit: Two hours *is* a normal commute for many modern business people.

▲ RULE #6:

The following indefinite words require singular verbs: *anybody, anyone, each, every, everyone, much, no one, one, other, somebody, something.*

Direct Hit: Everyone *learns* the basics of a language by the age of four.

▲ RULE #7:

These indefinite words require singular or plural verbs, depending on the meaning of the subject: *all, any, enough, most, some.*

Direct Hit: All she wants *is* to become CEO.

Direct Hit: All of her plans *are* aimed toward that goal.

▲ RULE #8:

A whole clause or phrase requires a singular verb:

Direct Hit: Combining the wine press and the coin punch *is* the way Johannes Gutenberg invented the printing press.

▲ RULE #9:

Some subjects refer to groups of people yet require singular verbs: *team, family, jury, crowd, class, committee.*

Direct Hit: The team from R and D *was* nicknamed the
                Widget Wizards of the West.

▲ RULE #10:

Some words with *-s* endings look plural but require singular verbs: *physics, mathematics, news, measles.*

Direct Hit: Even though mathematics *was* not one of
                Einstein's strengths, physics *was.*

▲ RULE #11:

Titles of written works, films, and other works of art require singular verbs as do names of companies and words referred to as words:

Direct Hit: *Writing: Research, Theory, and Application is* a
                valuable book for teachers of English.

Direct Hit: Procter and Gamble *is* known for requiring its
                employees to reduce lengthy reports to
                one-page memos.

Direct Hit: *Hopefully is* accepted as correct usage by some
                grammarians but condemned by others.

▲ RULE #12:

With *there is* and *there are,* the verb depends on what follows:

Direct Hit: *There are* 500,000 words in the English
                vocabulary, while in German *there are*
                185,000, and in French, only 100,000.

Direct Hit: *There is* one language in the world, English, with a vocabulary greater than that of German and French combined.

5. Wrong Word

Bad Swing: Creative people are different *than* uncreative people in a significant way.

Direct Hit: Creative people are different *from* uncreative people in a significant way.

Bad Swing: Creative people believe *their* creative.

Direct Hit: Creative people believe *they're* creative.

What's Wrong with Wrong Words?

This is a grab bag category of mistakes that follow few patterns. Some wrong words are simply misspellings of right words. For example, *a lot* should always be spelled as two words, not one. Other wrong words are new usages that haven't yet been accepted by grammarians. An example is *irregardless,* a word that is used so often that it will probably gain acceptance as the generation of anti-*irregardless* diehards dies out. (The correct version, by the way, is *regardless.*)

The problem is that most of the time, you don't even realize you're using one of those words incorrectly unless someone points it out. But, so what? That's a legitimate way to learn, so when it happens to you, look up the correct word in a dictionary and do the right thing.

I would ~~of~~ if I could ~~of~~.
have   have.

Rules of Thumb

▲ RULE #1:

Write first; edit later.

▲ RULE #2:

When in doubt, check it out. Use your dictionary or spell-checker to find out the correct spelling of any words you're not sure of.

▲ RULE #3:

Ask a picky, literate friend to proofread your writing. The biggest favor you can do for your grades in school or your position at the bank may be to find a trusted reader to catch the mistakes you miss.

Homonyms from Hell

Many wrong words belong to a category called homonyms, words that sound alike but are spelled differently, so writing them can trip you up (for example, *their* and *they're*). Some grammarians don't think it's smart to present these words as pairs because they claim that seeing them together can only add to the confusion.

I think they have a strong case, so I will separate several of the most common of these confused pairs and give examples of the correct use of each single word. This may

> seem strange at first, like the sound of one hand clapping, but I think you'll find it's a helping hand.

▲ RULE #4:

Remember that the following words are contractions.

it's   they're   you're   who's

it's = *it is* or *it has*
it is: It's a great day for grammar.
it has: It's been fun working with subject-verb agreement.

Think of the apostrophe in *it's* as a wedge that knocks the *i* out of *is* and the *ha* out of *has*.

they're = *they are*

> Creative people believe *they're* creative.

you're = *you are*

> Henry Ford claimed that whether you believe you can or you can't, *you're* right.

who's = *who is*

> In some conversations, you can't tell *who's* talking and *who's* listening.

Don't Look Back! Don't Look Back! You May Turn into a Pillar of Confused Pairs.
Well, maybe it wouldn't be that bad, but to test our hypothesis that the best way to unconfuse confused pairs is to study them separately, keep your eyes moving forward while we look at the other halves of the pairs.

▲ RULE #5:

Use the following possessive pronouns as adjectives, and don't confuse them with their hellacious homonyms (don't look back).

its   their   your   whose

its: A list of things to do loses *its* effectiveness if *its* items aren't done in order of priority.

their: People who tame *their* paper tigers deal with one document once only.

your: Mistakes in *your* résumé are time bombs in your job search.

whose: The introduction of dictionaries increased with the growth of the middle class, *whose* desire to copy the upper class included their pronunciation and spelling.

▲ RULE #6:

Remember that the following possessive pronouns don't require an apostrophe to show possession.

his   hers   yours   ours   theirs

Is this graffiti on my grammar book *his, hers,* or *yours?*

6. Missing Comma(s) with a Nonrestrictive Element

Bad Swing: Roger van Oech's *A Whack on the Side of the Head* expanded and revised for the 1990s is an excellent guide to a more creative life.

Direct Hit: Roger van Oech's *A Whack on the Side of the Head*, expanded and revised for the 1990s, is an excellent guide to a more creative life.

Bad Swing: *A Kick in the Seat of the Pants* also by von Oech is a valuable sequel to *A Whack on the Side of the Head.*

Direct Hit: *A Kick in the Seat of the Pants,* also by von Oech, is a valuable sequel to *A Whack on the Side of the Head.*

How to Punctuate Information that Is "Nice to Know"

For years, the definition of this mistake confused me, possibly because it was often paired with its opposite, Grammar's Top Miss #10, so I won't do that. What will I do? I'll give you the exciting news that a nonrestrictive element is a group of words or a word that isn't essential to the basic meaning of a sentence. A nonrestrictive element is written almost in the way a character in a play speaks an "aside" to the audience, adding information that's interesting but not absolutely essential. If you listen, you'll hear a slight pause before and after a nonessential element (or only before it if it occurs at the end of a sentence). In writing, these pauses are punctuated with commas.

Rules of
Thumb

▲ RULE #1:

Write first; edit later.

▲ RULE #2:

As a test, mentally omit the questionable element from the sentence. If the basic meaning of the sentence remains intact, then the element is nonessential, and it needs commas to set it off.

With the nonrestrictive (nonessential) element:

> Roger von Oech's *A Whack on the Side of the Head,* expanded and revised for the 1990s, is an excellent guide to a more creative life.

Omit the element:

> Roger von Oech's *A Whack on the Side of the Head* is an excellent guide to a more creative life.

(This version retains its basic meaning, so the added element is nonessential and needs commas to set it off.)

▲ RULE #3:

Read the sentence aloud. If you sense a pause before the element, then it is probably nonessential, so set it off with commas.

> *A Kick in the Seat of the Pants,* also by von Oech, is a valuable sequel to *A Whack on the Side of the Head.*

> If you can't find von Oech's books, however, try *Conceptual Blockbusting* by James Adams.

7. Unnecessary Shift in Tense

Bad Swing: The first English dictionary was published in 1604 and written by Robert Cawdray, who *says* he produced it for "ladies . . . and other unskillful persons."

Direct Hit: The first English dictionary was published in 1604 and written by Robert Cawdray, who *said* he produced it for "ladies . . . and other unskillful persons."

Bad Swing: In England and America, English speakers' attitudes toward correctness often *agree,* but their usage sometimes *differed.*

Direct Hit: In England and America, English speakers' attitudes toward correctness often *agree,* but their usage sometimes *differs.*

Tense Shifts

This category's title might make you think of learning to drive a stick shift in the hills of San Francisco, but what we're dealing with is simpler than that and much safer, too. *Tense* refers to the time during which the action of a verb takes place. We shift the tense of a verb correctly to show actions that occur at different times. Here's an example of a correct shift in tense:

> Someone named Murphy *said* that if something *can go* wrong, it *will.*

In that one sentence, you can see verbs used correctly in three different tenses: the past (*said*), the present (*can go*), and the future (*will*).

Tense shifts only become a problem when the meaning of your writing requires no shift:

(continued)

Bad Swing: I was walking through Disneyland when I *feel* the pavement start shaking under my feet.

Direct Hit: I was walking through Disneyland when I *felt* the pavement start shaking under my feet.

In the last example, since you were walking through Disneyland sometime in the past, you also *felt* the pavement shaking in the past.

Rules of Thumb

▲ RULE #1:

Write first; edit later.

▲ RULE #2:

Check your writing to make sure any shifts in verb tenses follow the time changes indicated by your meaning. In other words, it's all right to change from one tense to another if the actions you're describing happened at different times:

> O. J. Simpson *played* for the Buffalo Bills, but now he *works* for NBC.

However, if the actions occur at the same time, then stick to one tense:

> O. J. Simpson *played* for the Buffalo Bills and somehow *escaped* serious injury.

8. Missing Commas in a Series

Bad Swing: George Burns defines happiness as having a large loving caring close-knit family in another city.

Direct Hit: George Burns defines happiness as having a large, loving, caring, close-knit family in another city.

Bad Swing: Linguistic research has compared women to men in the same age groups social class and education level and has found that women take more care to speak standard English.

Direct Hit: Linguistic research has compared women to men of the same age, social class, and education and has found that women take more care to speak standard English.

Watch Out for Serial Commas

Ignoring serial commas can be dangerous. Make sure you use them to set off items in a series, or you might set off an unwanted reaction in your reader, boss, or teacher.

Rules of
Thumb

▲ RULE #1:

Write first; edit later.

▲ RULE #2:

Use commas to separate the following items in a series:

Words: George Burns defines happiness as having a
            large, loving, caring, close-knit family in
            another city.

Phrases: Wise time managers list their goals, order them
            by priority, and do something each day toward
            reaching them.

Clauses: Noah Webster began his career as a lawyer,
            then he turned to teaching and writing
            grammar books and spellers, and finally he
            produced his famous dictionaries.

9. Missing or Misplaced Possessive Apostrophe

Bad Swing: Parkinsons Law states that a job expands to fill the allotted time.

Direct Hit: Parkinson's Law states that a job expands to fill the allotted time.

Bad Swing: Shakespeares working vocabulary numbered over 30,000 words, while todays educated person uses about 15,000.

Direct Hit: Shakespeare's working vocabulary numbered over 30,000 words, while today's educated person uses about 15,000.

Possessive Apostrophe:
The Hooked Sign of Ownership

Think of the possessive apostrophe as a flashing neon sign telling you that the following word or word group belongs to the noun with the sign: Disneyland's Pirates of the Caribbean, Monique's Boutique. Even though the apostrophe has other uses, this is the one that causes the most mistakes, partly because you can't *hear* when an apostrophe is used. So, you just have to remember that a noun will need an apostrophe and some help from an s to show possession.

    Speaking of Disney pirates, you could also try thinking of a possessive apostrophe as Captain Hook's steel claw and the s as the hissing sound the captain makes as he hooks on to the lid of his treasure chest, warning all comers that thissss belongs to Hook!

Rules of Thumb

▲ RULE #1:
_____

Write first; edit later.

▲ RULE #2:
_____

To show possession, add **'s** to singular words:

Parkinson's Law   Shakespeare's working
                                vocabulary

Captain Hook's claw   today's educated person

▲ RULE #3:
_____

Add **'s** to plural words that don't end in s:

children's linguistic   the Women's Studies Program
   knowledge

the Men's Movement   three blind mice's tails

▲ RULE #4:

Add only an apostrophe to plural words ending in *s*:

English speakers' attitudes   English teachers' red pens

grammarians' disagreements   the widget wizards'
                             inventions

10. Unnecessary Comma(s) with a Restrictive Element

Bad Swing: Linguistic research has found, that New
               Yorkers communicate social class through
               their pronunciation of the letter *r*.

Direct Hit: Linguistic research has found that New Yorkers
               communicate social class through their
               pronunciation of the letter *r*.

Bad Swing: People, who exercise daily, feel more energetic
               than sedentary people.

Direct Hit: People who exercise daily feel more energetic
               than sedentary people.

**How to Punctuate Information
that Is "Need to Know"**
Think of a restrictive element as a word or word group
that is essential to the meaning of a sentence, just as a tight
belt, though restrictive, is essential to the meaning of a
pair of baggy trousers. Since these elements are essential,
they buckle up with the rest of the sentence without
pauses or commas. The Rules of Thumb will help you
avoid getting caught with your pants down.

Rules of Thumb

▲ RULE #1:

Write first; edit later.

▲ RULE #2:

To test whether or not an element is essential, leave it out and see if the basic meaning of the sentence is changed:

> With the element:

>> People who exercise daily feel more energetic than sedentary people.

> Without the element:

>> People feel more energetic than sedentary people.

Obviously, "who exercise daily" is essential to the meaning of the sentence, so it doesn't need commas to set it off.

▲ RULE #3:

Read the sentence out loud to hear if you pause before you read the word group. If there's no pause, usually there's no comma:

> Grammarians who try to keep new words out of English are often disappointed.

Of Kings and Commas

Notice how the addition of unnecessary commas can change the meaning of a sentence:

> The first Norman French king of England, who used English in official documents, was Henry V.

That sentence could mean that Henry V was the first Norman French king of England and that he used English in official documents. But we know that William the Conqueror was the first Norman French king of England, so something is wrong. Omit the commas and see how the meaning changes:

> The first Norman French king of England who used English in official documents was Henry V.

Now, without the commas, there is no implication that Henry V was the first Norman French king of England, only that he was the first of them to use English.

---

11. Confusion of *Its* and *It's*

Bad Swing: "If it sells, *its* creative," they say in advertising.

Direct Hit: "If it sells, *it's* creative," they say in advertising.

Bad Swing: A list of things to do loses *it's* effectiveness if *it's* items aren't done in order of priority.

Direct Hit: A list of things to do loses *its* effectiveness if *its*
items aren't done in order of priority.

Don't Say I Didn't Warn You

You're right. I did it. I just presented a confused pair
together, not because I wanted to, but because the research made me do it. *Its* and *it's* are confused so often
that they rate their own section in Grammar's Top 20. So
if seeing them together this way reconfuses you, don't
blame me. Just look at the Rules of Thumb for a quick
review. If you're still confused, go back to Grammar's Top
Miss #5, "Wrong Word," and deconfuse yourself.

**Rules of
Thumb**

▲ RULE #1:

Write first; edit later.

▲ RULE #2:

Remember that *it's* is a contraction of *it is.*

Direct Hit: *It's* confusing to study confused pairs together.

▲ RULE #3:

Remember that *its* is similar to *his* in that neither requires an apostrophe to show possession.

Direct Hit: The bear lost *its* tail fishing through a hole in the ice.

12. Dangling or Misplaced Modifier

Dangling Modifier:	*By the age of four,* the basic structures of a language have been learned unconsciously.
Direct Hit:	By the age of four, *children* have unconsciously learned the basic structures of a language.
Misplaced Modifier:	*Popping, sparking, and blowing fuses,* the CEO stood helplessly at the podium while the new audio-visual system self-destructed.
Direct Hit:	Popping, sparking, and blowing fuses, *the new audio-visual system self-destructed* while the CEO stood helplessly at the podium.

Haul 'Em Up, Place 'Em Right, and Move 'Em Out

A dangling modifier is a word or group of words that modifies something in a sentence, but we're not sure what, because the something isn't mentioned. In the example above, we needed to add *children* to the sentence in order to haul the dangling modifier into a meaningful position.

A misplaced modifier modifies the wrong word or words by being placed too close to them. In the above example, we needed to place the audio-visual system next to its fuses, not its CEO.

The Rules of Thumb will give you additional help in taking up slack and putting things in place.

Rules of Thumb

▲ RULE #1:

Write first; edit later.

▲ RULE #2:

To correct dangling modifiers, make sure you name the word modified, and place it near the modifier:

Dangling: *By the age of four,* the basic structures of a language have been learned unconsciously.

Direct Hit: By the age of four, *children* have unconsciously learned the basic structures of a language.

Dangling: *Worrying too much about mistakes,* writing can become a slow and painful process.

Direct Hit: If *you* worry too much about mistakes, writing can become a slow and painful process.

▲ RULE #3:

To correct a misplaced modifier, place the modifier as close as possible to the word or word group it modifies:

Misplaced: The airline's employees were told that their company was a victim of a hostile takeover *by their union representative.*

Direct Hit: The airline's employees were told *by their union representative* that their company was a victim of a hostile takeover.

Misplaced: *Racing to catch the bus,* a car just missed the commuter.

Direct Hit: Racing to catch the bus, *the commuter* was just missed by a car.

13. Lack of Agreement Between Pronoun and Antecedent

Bad Swing: A "Type-A" *person* will hurry *themselves* to death.

Direct Hit: A "Type-A" *person* will hurry *herself* or *himself* to death.

Direct Hit: "Type-A" *people* will hurry *themselves* to death.

Yet Another Disagreeable Part of Speech

This time the words that disagree are pronouns (*I, you, he, she, it, they*) and their antecedents (*Douglas, Cynthia, the bank, people, everyone*). Singular antecedents require singular pronouns, and plural antecedents require plural pronouns. As you will see, it's hard sometimes to keep the numbers straight.

Rules of Thumb

▲   RULE #1:

Write first; edit later.

▲ RULE #2:

When plural words come between a singular word and its pronoun, the pronoun still needs to be singular.

Bad Swing: *Each* of the "Type-A" *women* arranged *their* work so *they* could perform two tasks at the same time.

Direct Hit: *Each* of the "Type-A" *women* arranged *her* work so *she* could perform two tasks at the same time.

Avoiding the Sexist Use of *He*

Many disagreements between pronouns and their antecedents occur when we try to avoid using a masculine pronoun (*he, him, his*) to represent a general word such as *student.* This problem is a fairly recent one, as the use of *he* in place of singular antecedents was accepted practice, and in fact, was mandated by the British Parliament in 1850. However, we've come a long way, baby, since 1850, and this usage is actually prohibited by many government agencies today. The following Rules of Thumb suggest ways to avoid sexist language *and* mistakes.

▲ RULE #3:

With a singular antecedent, use both the feminine *and* masculine pronoun:

Sexist: The average college *student* will take more than 2,000 exams during *his* college career.

Nonsexist: The average college *student* will take more than 2,000 exams during *his* or *her* college career.

▲ RULE #4:
_____

Change singular antecedents to plural and use a plural pronoun:

Sexist: One linguistic study found that a Canadian will
                judge *his* fellow *countrymen* as less intelligent
                and less successful if they are French speakers.

Nonsexist: One linguistic study found that Canadians will
                judge *their* fellow *Canadians* as less intelligent
                and less successful if they are French speakers.

Hold on to Your Hats for This One
Rule #5 will be a shocker for many. To avoid the sexist
he, the National Council of Teachers of English allows the
use of the pronoun *they* to stand for a singular antecedent.
However, most English teachers still consider this use a
mistake, so if you want to play it safe, stick to rules three
and four.

▲ RULE #5:
_____

Use *they* to stand for a singular antecedent to avoid the sexist
use of the pronoun *he.*

Direct Hit: *Everybody* loves pizza, don't *they?*

Direct Hit: *Each* of the speakers created *their* own business.

Direct Hit: *Every* student handed in *their* work on time.

14. Wrong or Missing Preposition

Bad Swing: We need to invent a language in which
                politicians would be incapable *from* lying.

Direct Hit: We need to invent a language in which
                politicians would be incapable *of* lying.

Bad Swing: From rats in a maze to children in school, behavior tends to *comply to* the expectations of the observer.

Direct Hit: From rats in a maze to children in school, behavior tends to *comply with* the expectations of the observer.

Over the River and Through the Woods
Across the River and into the Trees

More than most mistakes, this one depends on local practice or idiom rather than on any fixed grammatical rules. You simply learn the use of prepositions as you hear and read English.

But we don't always learn the same usages. For example, I hear my son and his friends say they are bored *of* an activity, while I would say bored *with* it. How do we know which is correct? The Rules of Thumb will tell you where to go for an answer, but don't always expect to find one. I have looked up *bored* in the recommended references and haven't been able to find out if we should be bored *of, with,* or *by* a politician's speech (probably all three).

Still, if I were you, I wouldn't worry. If I can't find it, this one won't get you fired at the bank (or *from* or *by* the bank, either).

Rules of Thumb

▲ RULE #1:
_____

Write first; edit later.

▲ RULE #2:
_____

To find out which preposition goes with a word, look up the word in an unabridged dictionary. If you're lucky, it will provide a sample phrase or sentence with the word and the appropriate preposition:

> **ca•pa•ble** *adj.* 1. Having the capacity or qualities needed for: *capable of* good judgment.

**A Reference for the Serious
Seeker of Proper Prepositions**

If you are highly motivated to learn the last word on (or about) a preposition, look it up in *English Prepositional Idioms* by Frederick Wood, and you will see just how idiomatic our use of prepositions can be. Take, for example, the preposition *on. On* your way out of the kitchen, you can leave your briefcase *on* the stove, and it can catch *on* fire while you are talking *on* the phone. In that one sentence, you can see four different meanings of *on,* none determined by a rule. You learn these fine gradations of meaning unconsciously, and as in the case of wrong words, it takes a speaker of standard English to point out a nonstandard use.

If that happens to you, don't be embarrassed or shy. Do what any self-respecting citizen of the late 20th century would do. Put the blame on your parents, then join or establish a local chapter of Adult Children of Users of Nonstandard Prepositions.

---

15. Vague Pronoun Reference

Bad Swing: When making long-term decisions, some managers focus only on short-term profit, *which* can lower the quality of the product or service.

Direct Hit: When making long-term decisions, some managers focus only on short-term profit, and such a narrow focus can lower the quality of the product or service.

Bad Swing: The professor told her student that *she* needed a break from school.

Direct Hit: The professor told her student, "*I* need a break from school."

Who Did What to Whom, When, and Where?

A pronoun, as we know from previous sections, stands for another word or word group. When it isn't clear which word a pronoun refers to, we call this a vague pronoun reference, and if you have children or deal with children, this one is quite familiar:

> "He told him he was a jerk, and he pushed him, and he hit him in the stomach, and he ripped his shirt, but they only took *him* to the principal!" Whoa!

Most vague pronoun references fall into three categories, and we'll look at these common types in Rules of Thumb.

**Rules of
Thumb**

He started it!

▲ RULE #1:
_____

Write first; edit later.

▲ RULE #2:
_____

Show clearly which word the pronoun refers to:

Vague: The Zen master told the cognitive psychologist
              that *he* was losing *his* mind, but it didn't
              matter.

Direct Hit: The Zen master told the cognitive psychologist
              that *the psychologist* was losing *his* mind, but it
              didn't matter.

                              or

Direct Hit: The Zen master told the cognitive psychologist,
              "You are losing your mind, but it doesn't
              matter."

▲ RULE #3:
_____

Use the pronoun *who* to refer to persons.

Bad Swing: Professor W. E. Deming questions the value of
              rewarding employees *that* make fewer
              mistakes and punishing those *that* make more.

Direct Hit: Professor W. E. Deming questions the value of rewarding employees *who* make fewer mistakes and punishing those *who* make more.

▲ RULE #4:

When using a *which* clause, make sure you show clearly which noun(s) it refers to.

Bad Swing: In 1961, Merriam-Webster published a revised dictionary based on the principle of describing the way words are actually used rather than on the practice of prescribing the way they should be used, *which* caused what one linguist called a "war of the words" among grammarians.

Direct Hit: In 1961, Merriam-Webster published a revised dictionary based on the principle of describing the way words are actually used rather than on the practice of prescribing the way they should be used. This new focus caused what one linguist called a "war of the words" among grammarians.

In the above example, *which* refers to the new orientation of the dictionary, not to the act of publication.

16. Unnecessary Shift in Pronoun

Bad Swing: If *one* wants to become an international airline pilot, *they* have to learn English.

Direct Hit: If *you* want to become an international airline pilot, *you* have to learn English.

Bad Swing: Whether *we* expect good or poor performance from students, *one* gets what *they* are looking for.

Direct Hit: Whether *we* expect good or poor performance from students, *we* get what *we* are looking for.

Another Shifty Part of Speech

Many pronoun shifts occur when writers try to follow rigid rules about pronouns. If you are like many of my college students, your high school English teachers taught you not to use *I, we,* or *you* in your writing, and this prohibition can easily force you into the following unnecessary pronoun shift:

Unnecessary Shift: If *one* cannot use a wide range of pronouns, *they* end up making inappropriate pronoun shifts.

Direct Hit: If *we* cannot use a wide range of pronouns, *we* end up making inappropriate pronoun shifts.

And *déjà vu* all over again, the unnecessary pronoun shift often occurs when we're trying to avoid the sexist use of *he,* a problem we discussed in Grammar's Top Miss #13, Lack of Agreement Between Pronoun and Antecedent. Read the Rules of Thumb for some common pronoun shifts and ways to avoid them.

Rules of Thumb

▲ RULE #1:

Write first; edit later.

▲ RULE #2:

To avoid shifts between singular and plural pronouns, rewrite both in the plural:

Bad Shift: According to *What Color Is Your Parachute?*, a person who interviews a company is more successful in *their* job search than *one* who waits for a company to interview *them*.

Direct Hit: According to *What Color Is Your Parachute?*, people who interview companies are more successful in *their* job search than *those* who wait for a company to interview *them*.

▲ RULE #3:

Try breaking outmoded rules that prohibit the use of *I, you,* or *we* in your writing. It can provide a wild new experience.

Three direct hits:

Brave New We: *We* need to teach students to think critically, but *we* also need to teach them to think creatively.

Brave New You: According to Dr. Hans Selye, the only thing no one can take from *you* is what *you* can learn.

Brave New You and I: If *you* are a perfectionist (as *I* am),
then here's a valuable piece of advice:
Begin before *you* are ready.

17. Comma Splice (or Comma Fault)

Bad Swing: Professor Adams Sherman Hill of Harvard was
obsessed with mistakes in grammar, he passed
his obsession on to generations of English
teachers and the American public.

Direct Hit: Professor Adams Sherman Hill of Harvard was
obsessed with mistakes in grammar, *and* he
passed his obsession on to generations of
English teachers and the American public.

Bad Swing: Do what you love, the money will follow.

Direct Hit: Do what you love; the money will follow.

Strength of Punctuation 101

For some reason, someone in our history decided that a
comma couldn't join two independent clauses (or separate them adequately, depending on how you look at it).
It's as if we're dealing with a problem in strength of
materials, and the comma isn't strong enough to fasten
the joint. So, we have to bring Rosie the Riveter back from
World War II to slam in a period over the comma (pro-
ducing a "stronger" semicolon) or rivet a period in place
of the comma (creating two separate sentences).

Adding to the problem, in published writing, we often
see this use of the comma to separate two closely related
clauses, and like the proverbial monkey, we do what we
see. But, when in doubt, play it safe. Avoid the comma
splice in the ways suggested in Rules of Thumb.

Rules of Thumb

▲ RULE #1:

Write first; edit later.

▲ RULE #2:

Add a coordinating conjunction to go with the comma (*and, but, or, nor, for, so, yet*):

Direct Hit: W. E. Deming opposes merit pay for exceptional workers, *and* he claims it produces strife and tension among the unrewarded workers.

▲ RULE #3:

Replace the comma with a semicolon:

Direct Hit: W. E. Deming opposes merit pay for exceptional workers; he claims it produces strife and tension among the unrewarded workers.

▲ RULE #4:

Replace the comma with a period:

Direct Hit: W. E. Deming opposes merit pay for exceptional workers. He claims it produces strife and tension among the unrewarded workers.

▲ RULE #5:

Change one of the clauses to a *because* clause:

Direct Hit: W. E. Deming opposes merit pay for exceptional workers *because* he claims it produces strife and tension among the unrewarded workers.

18. Wrong or Missing Verb Ending

Bad Swing: The healthy office worker *park* one mile from work and *walk* twenty minutes for exercise.

Direct Hit: The healthy office worker *parks* one mile from work and *walks* twenty minutes for exercise.

Bad Swing: Someone *ask* T. S. Eliot if he *agree* that all editors are failed writers. "Yes," he said, "but so are all writers."

Direct Hit: Someone *asked* T. S. Eliot if he *agreed* that all editors are failed writers. "Yes," he said, "but so are all writers."

How the Verb Lost Its Tail

This happens when we drop an *-s* or an *-ed* ending from a verb. People who make this mistake have grown up hearing a dialect of English that omits these verb endings, or they first learned a language like Chinese that doesn't have verb tenses. For them, it takes longer to learn the correct verb forms.

Rules of Thumb

▲ RULE #1:

Write first; edit later.

▲ RULE #2:

If you omit verb endings consistently, call on your picky, literate friend again and ask for proofreading help.

▲ RULE #3:
_____

Read a lot. That's right. Reading books, magazines, or newspapers for pleasure will help you correct this mistake by training your eye and subconscious mind with a thousand versions of the correct forms.

19. Missing Comma in a Compound Sentence

Bad Swing: People who follow the 80/20 rule begin working on the most important aspects of a project and they often can skip the remaining tasks.

Direct Hit: People who follow the 80/20 rule begin working on the most important aspects of a project, and they often can skip the remaining tasks.

Bad Swing: Many Americans own a thesaurus yet such books of synonyms don't exist for some languages with small vocabularies.

Direct Hit: Many Americans own a thesaurus, yet such books of synonyms don't exist for some languages with small vocabularies.

**Love and Marriage Go Together Like a
Comma and a Coordinating Conjunction**
This mistake isn't as frequent as divorce, nor is it as serious, and when it happens, it's not as hard on the kids. However, we have to deal with it as an unpleasant fact of our society. You can correct it by simply remarrying the comma with the coordinating conjunction it should precede (*and, or, for, but, nor, so, yet*).

Rules of Thumb

▲ RULE #1:

Write first; edit later.

▲ RULE #2:

When two independent clauses are joined by a coordinating conjunction, place a comma before the conjunction:

Direct Hit: Deming management theory points to cooperation as a more effective force than competition, and corporations like Ford Motors now take this orientation seriously.

Direct Hit: In English, many nouns can double as verbs, and many verbs can become nouns.

20. Missing Comma After an Introductory Element

Bad Swing: While the dog ate the cat stayed away from the dish.

Direct Hit: While the dog ate, the cat stayed away from the dish.

Bad Swing: Before 1600 if you had told educated people in England that there was only one way to spell a word they would have laughed at you.

Direct Hit: Before 1600, if you had told educated people in England that there was only one way to spell a word, they would have laughed at you.

The Missing Comma that Few of Us Miss

Of the twenty most common mistakes we make in English, this one is committed most often, yet it causes the weakest negative response from readers. So why bother with it? First, it is sometimes necessary to prevent confusion (while the dog ate, the cat . . .). And second, there are still a few comma sleuths out there who are offended by this mistake, so it's nice to know what to do when apprehended.

Rules of Thumb

▲ RULE #1:

Write first; edit later.

▲ RULE #2:

Use a comma after introductory elements when its absence would cause confusion:

Confusing: When you are writing grammar rules can interrupt the flow of your thoughts.

Direct Hit: When you are writing, grammar rules can interrupt the flow of your thoughts.

▲ RULE #3:

Use a comma after introductory words when you hear a pause:

Direct Hit: In fact, some psychologists call Type-A behavior the "Hurry Disease."

▲ RULE #4:

Use a comma after four or more introductory words:

Direct Hit: When Thomas Jefferson coined *belittle,* the word was not at first accepted as correct usage.

7

Five Uncommonly Serious Mistakes

▼▼▼▼▼▼▼▼▼

A Rare and Dangerous Breed

The next (and final) 5 mistakes are not common enough to rate on Grammar's Top 20 Misses, but when you make them, they cause a strong negative reaction in the great majority of readers. So, it's worth your time and effort to make sure you *don't* make them.

If these mistakes cause no problems for you, then forget I ever mentioned them. If any do present a problem, then use the Rules of Thumb to drive this rare species into extinction.

---

1. Objective Case Pronouns Used as Subjects

Bad Swing: Her guru and *her* agreed that we are what we think.

Direct Hit: Her guru and *she* agreed that we are what we think.

Bad Swing: We were all surprised to learn that Shakespeare coined more than 2,000 words, but no one was more surprised than *me.*

Direct Hit: We were all surprised to learn that Shakespeare coined more than 2,000 words, but no one was more surprised than *I.*

The Case of the Erroneous Case

Mistakes like this are often blamed on the idioms or dialects we learned as children. But anyone who deals with children will notice that they all use constructions like, "Me and Nick went to the beach," regardless of the way their parents speak. So, blame it on the neighbors. Then refer to Rules of Thumb to cure the whole family.

Rules of Thumb

▲ RULE #1:

Write first; edit later.

▲ RULE #2:

Test the correct form of the pronoun by using it alone with the verb:

Bad Swing: Her guru and *her* agreed that we are what we think.

Test: . . . *her* agreed that we are what we think.

or

. . . *she* agreed that we are what we think.

Bingo! If you said *she agreed* is correct, *you're* correct. If not, stay away from the neighbors and try again.

Direct Hit: Her guru and *she* agreed that we are what we think.

Bad Swing: Nick and *me* went to the beach.

Test: . . . *me* went to the beach.

or

. . . *I* went to the beach.

Direct Hit: Nick and *I* went to the beach.

▲ RULE #3:
_____

When sentences end with the following pronoun construction, add a verb as the test:

Bad Swing: We were all surprised to learn that Shakespeare coined more than 2,000 words, but no one was more surprised than *me*.

Test: Add the verb (in this case, *was*) that is understood to go with *me*.

. . . no one was more surprised than *me* was.

or

. . . no one was more surprised than *I* was.

Direct Hit: We were all surprised to learn that Shakespeare coined more than 2,000 words, but no one was more surprised than *I*.

Bad Swing: E. B. White was more erudite than *me*.

Test: . . . more erudite than *me* am.

                            or

                . . . more erudite than *I* am.

Direct Hit: E. B. White was more erudite than *I.*

2. Double Negatives

Bad Swing: One hard lesson for many to learn is that worry *won't hardly* change the future.

Direct Hit: One hard lesson for many to learn is that worry *hardly* changes the future.

                            or

Direct Hit: One hard lesson for many to learn is that worry *won't* change the future.

Bad Swing: Poverty *won't* make *no* good hedge against inflation.

Direct Hit: Poverty *won't* make a good hedge against inflation.

Double Your Pleasure, Double Your Fun,
but Don't Double Your Negatives
Several dialects of English allow the use of the double negative, and certain languages (French for one) even allow double negatives in their standard forms. In fact, so did English until some grammarian in the 17th century ruled against it, and the rule stuck. Now the double negative strikes many ears as uneducated, and yes, even criminal. So check it out in Rules of Thumb, and proof-read your writing for double negatives if you want to stay out of the grammar slammer.

Rules of Thumb

▲ RULE #1:

Write first; edit later.

▲ RULE #2:

When using words with a "built-in" negative (such as *scarcely, hardly, never, neither*), avoid using additional negatives (such as *no, not, can't, don't*):

Double Negative: On weekends, the wise worker *doesn't never* think of work.

Direct Hit: On weekends, the wise worker *never* thinks of work.

▲ RULE #3:

When using a contraction of *not* (*isn't, doesn't, can't*), avoid using additional negatives:

Double Negative: Mark Twain felt that since we *can't hardly* keep people from lying, we should teach them to lie with style and grace.

Direct Hit: Mark Twain felt that since we *can't* keep people from lying, we should teach them to lie with style and grace.

Don't Say It Ain't Not So, Joe
Standard English does allow the use of the double negative to express an *affirmative* thought: "These hills are *not unlike* the hills of Scotland." But this use can cause confusion, so play it safe and avoid it. See Rule #4.

▲ RULE #4:
_____

To avoid confusion, recast negative statements in the affirmative:

Correct but Confusing: *No* language exists in which you *cannot* lie.

Direct Hit: You can lie in any language.

3. Failure to Capitalize Proper Names

Bad Swing: Unlike the *french, spanish, italians,* and *germans,* the *english* never established an official academy to standardize their language.

Direct Hit: Unlike the French, Spanish, Italians, and Germans, the English never established an official academy to standardize their language.

Bad Swing: *roger* von *oech,* the president of *creative think,* has conducted seminars in creativity for *american express, apple computer, procter* and *gamble,* and the *japanese management association.*

Direct Hit: Roger von Oech, the president of *Creative Think,* has conducted seminars in creativity for American Express, Apple Computer,

Procter and Gamble, and the Japanese Management Association.

FROM BRUTUS to the bauhaus—Capital Ideas

The history of capitalization is one of extremes. EARLY LATIN WAS WRITTEN ENTIRELY IN THE UPPER CASE, while the Bauhaus design movement in Germany tried to eliminate the use of capitals entirely, no small reform when you consider the fact that *all* nouns in German are capitalized.

English lies somewhere between these two extremes, with a few exceptions thrown in for bad measure. The Rules of Thumb will cover most cases, but when in doubt, you can find the answers to your capital questions by looking up words in a dictionary.

Rules of Thumb

▲ RULE #1:

Write first; edit later.

▲ RULE #2:

Capitalize the names of people:

General Norman Schwarzkopf	Barbara Bush
Madonna	Hulk Hogan
Lamar Alexander	Janice Gallagher
Betsy Amster	Carl Lewis

▲ RULE #3:

Capitalize specific place names and geographical areas:

Hot Coffee, Mississippi	Asia
the South	Japan
Wall Street	Bad Axe, Michigan

▲ RULE #4:

Capitalize the names of nationalities, races, and their languages:

Arab—Arabic	Iranian—Farsi
French—French	Spaniard—Spanish
Israeli—Hebrew	Pakistani—Urdu

▲ RULE #5:

Capitalize the names of organizations and institutions:

American Cancer Society	United States Senate
Vanderbilt University	Rotary Club

▲ RULE #6:

Capitalize the names of religions, their deities, followers, and holy books:

Islam—Moslems—the Koran
Christianity—Christians—the Bible
Judaism—Jews—the Talmud

▲ RULE #7:

Capitalize the names of historical events and documents:

the Great San Francisco Earthquake   the Constitution
the Vietnam War   the Mayflower
                                       Compact

▲ RULE #8:

Capitalize days, holidays, and months (but not seasons):

Friday   July
Labor Day   (but spring, summer,
                                       fall, winter)

▲ RULE #9:

Capitalize trademarks and trade names:

Ford Motors   Kmart
New Balance   Sharp Products

4. Faulty Parallelism

Bad Swing: A good manager requires the ability to lead, the capacity to learn, and *delegating.*

Direct Hit: A good manager requires the ability to lead, the capacity to learn, and the willingness *to delegate.*

Bad Swing: W. E. Deming's management theory is expressed in what he labels the Fourteen Points, the Seven Deadly Diseases, and *how to eliminate* the Obstacles.

Direct Hit: W. E. Deming's management theory is expressed in what he labels the Fourteen Points, the Seven Deadly Diseases, and the Obstacles.

Geometric Grammar

Teachers of English composition advise us to vary the length and style of sentences to avoid monotony in our writing. However, within a single sentence, they like to see equal ideas expressed consistently in similar grammatical forms. Especially when the ideas are presented in a series, list, or comparison, they insist that we follow the rules of parallelism, a convention that sounds as though it belongs in geometry rather than in English. However, breaking the rule is considered a serious mistake, so look at the Rules of Thumb and follow the straight and narrow path of parallel structure.

Rules of Thumb

▲ RULE #1:

Write first; edit later.

▲ RULE #2:

Use parallel grammatical structures to express equal ideas:

Direct Hit: Three constants of modern life are *change, change,* and *change.*

Direct Hit: Dr. Hans Selye advised us *to increase* positive stressors in our lives, *to decrease* negative stressors, and *to find* the stress levels that work best for each of us.

▲ RULE #3:

Use parallel structures with comparative expressions:

both . . . and   *either . . . or*
not only *. . . but also*   *neither . . . nor*

Direct Hit: Not only are we *learning* grammar, but we are also *having* fun.

Direct Hit: Either *use* parallel constructions, or *face* the consequences.

5. Subjective Pronouns Used for Objects

Bad Swing: The senator's use of the double negative surprised my students and *I.*

Direct Hit: The senator's use of the double negative surprised my students and *me.*

Bad Swing: The producer told my agent and *I* that we would "do lunch" sometime soon.

Direct Hit: The producer told my agent and *me* that we would "do lunch" sometime soon.

Hypercorrection

No, this isn't a new program for your computer. It's a name for the tendency we have to overcorrect for mistakes by generalizing a rule to a situation where it doesn't apply. In the case of *I* and *me*, our parents and teachers corrected us when we said, "Me and Mary went to the store," telling us to say instead, "Mary and I," which was correct for the use of *I* as the subject of a sentence.

However, in our all-too-human desire to keep things regular, we often us *I* where *me* is correct. For instance, "between you and *I*" should be "between you and *me*" because *me* is the object of the preposition *between*. The Rules of Thumb provide an antidote to our overzealous application of our parents' prescription.

Rules of Thumb

▲ RULE #1:

Write first; edit later.

▲ RULE #2:

To test which form of the pronoun is correct, use it without the noun or pronoun it is paired with:

Bad Swing: The senator's use of the double negative surprised my students and *I.*

Test: The senator . . . surprised *I.*

or

The senator . . . surprised *me.*

Direct Hit: The senator's use of the double negative surprised my students and *me.*

Bad Swing: The producer finally invited my agent and *I* to lunch.

Test: The producer invited *I* . . .

or

The producer invited *me* . . .

Direct Hit: The producer finally invited my agent and *me* to lunch.

8

Spelling Is a Four-Letter Word

▼▼▼▼▼▼▼▼

80/20 Spelling—Bad News and Good News

First the Bad News

As we learned earlier in this book, English boasts the largest vocabulary of any language in the world. Estimates of how large vary, but the latest *Oxford English Dictionary* with supplements contains more than 600,000 entries, and the language is still growing at a heady rate. So, we poor English speakers simply have to learn how to spell a greater number of words than anyone else.

English isn't the most regular language to spell, either. For example, Albert Baugh and Thomas Cable have found 14 different ways to spell the *sh* sound in English: "*shoe, sugar, issue, mansion, mission, nation, suspicion, ocean, nauseous, conscious, chaperon, schist, fuchsia,* and *pshaw*" (*A History of the English Language,* page 12). Grammarians disagree about how irregular English spelling is, but you and I will probably agree that it's irregular enough to cause problems for anyone who has to write and spell it.

In fact, most people make spelling errors, and plenty of them. Andrea Lunsford and Robert Connors found that for every mistake we make in grammar, we commit 3 spelling errors (*The St. Martin's Handbook*, page xxxv.) That's right, folks, 3 to 1. Since you just learned 20 of the most common grammar mistakes, does this mean you'll have to learn *60* of the most common types of spelling errors and how to avoid them? You could try, but I wouldn't want to bet on your success. And, anyway, with our 80/20 orientation, would it even be worth your effort? That's where the good news comes in.

The Good News

In order to avoid mistakes in spelling, you don't have to learn 60 spelling rules, or 20, or even 1. You just need to learn how to use spelling resources that will help you find a correct spelling quickly and efficiently. So, for the time being, forget about putting i before e except after c, changing y to i and adding e-d, dropping or keeping a terminal e, or ending a word with -ally or -ly.

If you haven't learned these rules by now, maybe you never will, and maybe you won't need to. But just because you haven't learned auto mechanics, it doesn't mean you can't drive, does it? So get behind the spelling wheel and crank up the engine. In the following Rules of Thumb, you'll learn how to drive out those nocks and peengs while getting the best mileage and taking the least gas from spelling (Spelling Tune-Up: knocks and pings).

Rules of Thumb

▲ RULE #1:

Write first; edit later.

This rule may sound familiar, but you need to remember it now, because the temptation to stop writing and look up the spelling of a word is a powerful one, more easily succumbed to than hard drink and the opposite sex. Those spelling detours can be costly, especially if you forget your next idea while you're hunting for the right way to spell a word.

▲ RULE #2:

Use printed resources to look up correct spellings:

Dictionaries: Just about any dictionary will contain the words you normally use, although if you're into $100 words, you may need an unabridged dictionary, a *big* one with more words than the average bear.

Spelling Dictionaries: Some dictionaries exist solely for the purpose of helping you spell. They list commonly misspelled words without any definitions, so they are smaller and handier to use.

The Problem with Dictionaries

If you have severe problems with spelling, dictionaries may not offer much help. For example, if you spell by ear, you might think that *photograph* is spelled *fotograf*. Looking for *fotograf* in a standard dictionary could keep you in the *f*'s for much longer than the 80/20 rule allows.

Fortunately, some dictionaries tackle this problem by listing common misspellings in a column beside the correct spelling. This way, you can look up *fotograph* in the *f*'s and find *photograph* in the column beside it. One speller that does this is *How to Spell It* by Harriet Wittels and Joan Greisman. Electronic spell-checkers do the same thing, only more quickly (see Rule #3).

▲ RULE #3:
_____

Use electronic resources for spelling.

The wacky, wonderful world of electronics is coming to our rescue day by day with new devices to help us spell. First, there's a spell-check function in word processing programs that will tell you if you have spelled a word incorrectly and then correct it for you. Then, there's a variety of spell-checking instruments, small boxes the size of hand-held video games that allow you to key in the incorrect spelling of a word (*fotograf*) and see the correct version on a one-word screen (*photograph*).

A small drawback to any form of spell-checker is that it can tell if a word is spelled correctly, but not if it's used in the wrong place. For example, if you are using *there* when you should have used one of its hellacious homonyms (Don't look back!), the spell-checker will only know that you have spelled *there* correctly, not that you should be using *they're* or *their*. In spite of that small drawback, electronic spell-checking is a great help. Use it.

▲ RULE #4:
_____

Use human resources for spelling.

If you're a poor speller, find a good speller to proofread your writing. Remember, if your car is having engine problems, you don't need to *become* a mechanic to fix it, you just need to *call* one. A similar approach to spelling will free you to devote your time to your strengths and the speller to his or hers.

A footnote for parents: If your child asks you how to spell a word, don't say, "Look it up." If you know the correct spelling, shout it out! Writing is hard enough for most kids, and anything that makes it harder will make them hate it. And if they hate it, they will avoid anything that requires it, as we know from the majority of UCLA students who have avoided courses, majors, or careers that require writing.

What About School or Work Settings that Require Writing Without These Spelling Resources?

I'm glad you asked. If you're taking a course and have to write in class, ask the teacher to let you use a dictionary, spell-checker, or lap-top computer. Most teachers will cooperate, but one word of warning (actually, four words): Write first; spell-check later. Don't interrupt the flow of your ideas to look up spellings. Get your ideas down first; then go back and check for misspelled words.

If you're giving a business presentation or teaching a class that requires spontaneous writing in front of a group, start off by explaining you're a poor speller, and then enlist the aid of a good speller from the audience. Good spellers are proud of their ability and like to be singled out. So help their egos and yours: Say it loud! You can't spell and you're proud!

▲ RULE #5:

A short tip for long-term spelling improvement: Read for pleasure.

For most of us, *seeing* words over and over again will provide all the spelling practice we need. So read a lot for pleasure, with the emphasis on *pleasure*. Whether you read *People, Popular Mechanics,* or *Your Personal Best,* racy romance, futuristic fantasy, or hairy horror, you are seeing thousands of words spelled correctly and learning how to spell them without consciously trying, just as you learned how to speak by listening to people talk in your everyday world.

This approach may not appeal to people who believe you have to work hard to learn how to spell, people I call the Puritans of spelling. One definition of a Puritan is a person who fears that someone, somewhere is having a good time. Well, believe it or not, you can learn to spell *while* you're

having a good time, so read, improve your spelling, and have
fun doing it.

Spel Is a Four-Letter Word

Spel Is a Four-Letter Word is the title of a book by Richard
Gentry, Ph.D., director of the Reading Center at Western
Carolina University. In the book, Gentry tells the story of
how he won numerous spelling contests as a child, but a
few days after each contest, he had already forgotten one
quarter of the spellings he had memorized.

Though a good writer, Gentry never became a "good"
speller, and like many people who have a problem, he
decided to devote his professional life to finding its causes
and possible cures. So, he earned a Ph.D. in Education at
the University of Virginia (he says he has a Ph.D. in
spelling) and specialized in the study of how we learn to
spell.

What did Gentry find out? First, that learning to spell
follows a natural process like the one we go through when
we learn to speak. Just as children begin speaking by
babbling sounds that gradually approximate the exact
sounds of the words they hear, if left to their own devices,
they will begin writing by scribbling and then writing
words that gradually approximate the exact spellings of
the words they hear and (later) read.

Unfortunately, Gentry also found that the traditional
school approach to spelling interrupts this developmental
process by placing an undue emphasis on correct spelling,
transforming writing into a painful and even dangerous
chore for many children.

Finally, Gentry confirmed his own experience that
some people will never be able to spell as well as others,
and they shouldn't be punished for an inherited glitch in

(continued)

their perceptual memory. After all, no one gives us bad grades because we can't run as fast as Carl Lewis or Florence Griffith-Joyner. Likewise, if you are a "slow" speller, you need to relax your own self-grading, accept your spelling as it is, and provide yourself access to the spelling resources described above.

9

Where Do You Go from Here?

▼▼▼▼▼▼▼▼▼

Breaking Out of the Grammar Slammer

If we can believe research, over three quarters of our college students avoid courses, majors, or careers that require writing. This means that many educated Americans are trapped in a prison that keeps them from reaching their full professional potential. It's a prison whose foundations are laid by well-meaning teachers and parents who respond too often to how you spell and punctuate, and too seldom to the message contained in your writing. The walls of the prison are erected and patrolled by members of a society and business world whose first response to writing is to point out mistakes in grammar and spelling. And finally, the walls are maintained by each of us when we focus on grammar and spelling in the early stages of a writing task.

So, how do you break out of the grammar slammer? After reading this book, many of you have taken the first step toward freedom by gaining more confidence in your correct use of the language. You now think more about *what* you are writing and less about how correctly it is written. Do I mean to say that you can make it in school or work with writing that's full of mistakes? No. What I mean is that some of you have learned to write first and edit later, freeing yourself to do a better job of each.

Unfortunately, for some of you, one effect of reading

(continued)

this book may be to increase your fear of making mistakes, building the walls of your prison even higher. Paradoxically, some research has found that the more we focus on mistakes, the more mistakes we make. To ensure that effect is not a lasting one, I want to leave you with a few tips in the final Rules of Thumb that will help you escape for good the imprisoning fear of grammar.

Rules of Thumb

▲ RULE #1:

Write first; edit later.

By now I've repeated this rule at least 25 times, but guess what, it's still true. The less you think about correct grammar and spelling while you're getting your ideas on paper, the better you'll write.

Give yourself permission to make mistakes in your first draft, and just say what you have to say. Then come back later with your fine-clawed grammar hammer and pull out the mistakes. If you have trouble locating them, proceed to rule 2.

▲ RULE #2:

Find a grammar accomplice.

Just as some people spell well, others swing a mean grammar hammer. Enlist one of these heavy hitters on your side, especially if you have problems even recognizing the mistakes you make. Helpers come in various forms. I've listed the basic types below:

▲ Friends at school or work.

Find someone who is willing to correct your writing before you do a final draft. You could offer to return the favor in some way or even pay for their time. However you work it out, such an arrangement will work to your benefit.

▲ The English department of your local college or university.

Call the department office and ask for the names of graduate students who will edit your writing for a fee. Many starving students can do more than move furniture, and often their work will rival that of professional editors.

▲ Professional typing or editing services.

Look in your Yellow Pages under *editing, editors, typing, word processing,* and any other entries you can think of. Check out what services are available and what they cost. Then take a short piece of your writing to several different people and see who does the best work. You may not want to spend money on something you feel you *ought* to be able to do yourself, but spending a few dollars on that special report may turn out to be money in the bank, especially if you want to keep working there.

▲ School writing centers.

Most colleges and some high schools operate special writing centers where faculty and student tutors will help you with anything from initial brainstorming to final editing. If you're a student, and your school has a writing center, use it.

▲ RULE #3:
_____

Read for pleasure.

Yes, I've also said this before, but I'll say it again with a final twist. Remember, you don't have to read the classics to improve your writing. What's a classic? Mark Twain defined it as a work that everyone wants to have read, but one that no one wants to read. Luckily, you don't have to read "great literature" to improve your use of English. Instead you can read newspapers, magazines, history, or horror.

One additional piece of advice about reading: As well as reading for fun, read the types of writing you plan to write. Ask teachers for sample papers, bosses for sample reports. When you want to improve your tennis game, it helps to watch pro matches. The same goes in the game of writing.

▲ RULE #4:

Practice sentence combining.

Over the past 20 years, a new method for improving sentence structure and punctuation has been found to work. It involves exercises that require you to make big sentences out of little ones, and what's best, you learn principles of grammar and punctuation without having to learn any terms. There are several sentence-combining books on the market, any of which will work. In my classes, I use William Strong's text, entitled appropriately enough, *Sentence Combining,* and I recommend it to you.

Hammertime!
Remember the English teacher I mentioned in Who's Afraid of the Grammar Hammer?, someone you met at a party who made you worry that you might make mistakes in grammar as you spoke? Let's put a face on that figure. Imagine a college teacher, male, 48, balding, average height, overweight but solid, wearing a suit and tie and a serious look. To top it all off, the person who introduces you says (just before walking away and leaving you alone with the teacher), "Douglas just finished writing a grammar book."

How do you feel now? Well, after reading *Under the Grammar Hammer,* I hope you'd feel less nervous than you would have felt before reading it. I hope you now feel more confident in your use of grammar, and that your attitude toward grammar and its teachers has changed. This guy doesn't *own* the language, does he? Who is he to make you nervous about using your own language? That's the spirit.

Just to make sure that you finish the book in the right frame of mind, I'm going to make a final switch in the meaning of *grammar hammer.* Instead of a steel-headed, wooden-handled tool that bashes thumbs if swung incorrectly, I want you to visualize the amazing, dancing, singing, master of rap, *Hammer!* Then, I'd like you to transform the stereotype of the English teacher (yes, I have to admit, it's me, rather it is I, the author of this book). Instead of the suit and tie, dress him in a pair of oversized Hammer pants. You know the kind: red silk balloon pants with the legs joined down to the knees and tight around the ankles. That's it. Picture him as a kind of balding, blue-eyed, lightweight sumo wrestler in Hammer pants. Now, how can you take a guy like that seriously?

Okay. Next step. Whenever you meet English teachers or any other self-appointed guardians of the language, mentally dress them in Hammer pants. Picture them dancin', rappin', droppin' the *g*'s from their *ing*'s, sayin' *ain't* and *it don't mean nothin'.* Havin' fun.

Finally, whenever you have to write for school or work, slide into your own pair of "Grammar" Hammer pants, and dance your way through your first draft. Got it? Okay. Let's practice:

(continued)

Hammertime! Watch Me Dance!

It's been 500 years since 1492,
When old Chris Columbus sailed the ocean so blue,
And a monk in Spain wrote the first book of grammar,
That started all the trouble that can land us in the
    slammer.
But we don't have to worry 'bout our commas and our
    spelling,
'Cause we got a new book (and I hope by now it's selling).
We know the Top 20 and the 5 Uncommon bad ones,
And a mean grammar hammer can no longer make us sad
    ones,
'Cause D. C. "Grammar" Hammer shows us how to dance,
And the new Grammar Hammer wears a baggy pair of
    pants.

My apologies to my fellow teachers of English, to Hammer,
and to all lovers of rap.

Good luck, and good grammar.

Bibliography

▼▼▼▼▼▼▼▼▼

Aguayo, Rafael. *Dr. Deming.* New York: Fireside, 1990.

Batholomae, David. "The Study of Error." *College Composition and Communication* 31 (1980): 253–69.

Baugh, Albert, and Thomas Cable. *A History of the English Language.* Englewood Cliffs, N.J.: Prentice-Hall, 1978.

Bryson, Bill. *The Mother Tongue: English And How It Got To Be That Way.* New York: William Morrow, 1990.

Copperud, Roy. *American Usage and Style: The Consensus.* New York: Van Nostrand, 1980.

Farb, Peter. *Word Play.* New York: Knopf, 1974.

Finnegan, Edward. *Attitudes Toward English Usage: The History of a War of Words.* New York: Teachers College Press, 1980.

Friedmann, Thomas. "Teaching Error, Nurturing Confusion: Grammar Texts, Tests, and Teachers in the Developmental English class." *College English* 45.5 (1983): 390–399.

Gentry, J. R. *Spel Is a Four-Letter Word.* Portsmouth, N.H.: Heinemann, 1987.

Gorrell, Donna. "Controlled Composition for Basic Writers." *College Composition and Communication* 32 (1981): 308–316.

Greenbaum, Sidney, and John Taylor. "The Recognition of Usage Errors by Instructors of Freshman Composition." *College Composition and Communication* 32 (1981): 169–74.

Hairston, Maxine. "Not All Errors Are Created Equal; Nonacademic Readers in the Professions Respond to Lapses in Usage." *College English* 43.8 (1981): 794–806.

Harris, Muriel, and Katherine E. Rowan. "Explaining Grammatical Concepts." *Journal of Basic Writing* 8.2 (1989): 21–41.

Hartwell, Patrick. "Grammar, Grammars, and the Teaching of Grammar." *College English* 47.2 (1985): 105–127.

Jochnowitz, George. "Everybody Likes Pizza, Doesn't He or She?" *American Speech* 57.5 (1982): 198–203.

Lunsford, Andrea, and Robert Connors. *The St. Martin's Handbook: Annotated Instructor's Edition.* New York: St. Martin's, 1989.

McCrum, Robert, William Cran, and Robert McNeil. *The Story of English.* New York: Viking, 1986.

Tennyson, Robert. "Pictorial Support and Specific Instructors as Design Variables for Children's Concept and Rule Learning." *Educational Communication and Technology* 26.4 (1978): 291–99.

von Oech, Roger. *A Kick in the Seat of the Pants.* New York: Harper and Row, 1986.

———. *A Whack on the Side of the Head.* 2nd ed. New York: Warner, 1990.

Wall, Susan, and Glynda Hull. "The Semantics of Error: What Do Teachers Know?" *Writing and Response: Theory, Practice, and Research.* Ed. Chris Anson. Urbana, Illinois: NCTE, 1989. 261–92.

Walton, Mary. *Deming Management at Work.* New York: Perigee Books, 1990.

Williams, Joseph. "The Phenomenology of Error." *College Composition and Communication* 32 (1981): 152–68.

Wittels, Harriet, and Joan Greisman. *How to Spell It.* New York: Grosset and Dunlap, 1973.

Wood, Frederick. *English Prepositional Idioms.* New York: St. Martin's Press, 1967.

Index

▼▼▼▼▼▼▼▼▼▼